JOSEPH HAYDN
Complete Piano Sonatas

IN TWO VOLUMES

VOLUME II
(*Hoboken Nos. 30–52*)

DOVER PUBLICATIONS, INC.
NEW YORK

This Dover edition in two volumes, first published in 1984, contains all the music from
the three volumes comprising *Serie 14: Klavierwerke* [1918] of the complete-works edition
Joseph Haydns Werke. Erste kritisch durchgesehene Gesamtausgabe, published by Breitkopf &
Härtel, Leipzig, 1907 ff. The table of contents and Publisher's Note have been prepared
specially for the present edition; see the Publisher's Note for further bibliographical
information.

Manufactured in the United States of America
Dover Publications, Inc., 31 East 2nd Street, Mineola, N.Y. 11501

Library of Congress Cataloging-in-Publication Data

Haydn, Joseph, 1732–1809.
  [Sonatas, piano]
  Complete piano sonatas.

  Reprint: Originally published: Leipzig : Breitkopf & Härtel, 1918 (Joseph Haydns
Werke. Erste kritisch durchgesehene Gesamtausgabe, Serie 14: Klavierwerke / edited by
Karl Päsler).
  Contents: v. 1. Hoboken nos. 1–29 — v. 2. Hoboken nos. 30–52.
  1. Sonatas (Piano) I. Päsler, Karl.
M23.H41P33 1984   84-759555
ISBN 0-486-24726-0 (v. 1)
ISBN 0-486-24727-9 (v. 2)

PUBLISHER'S NOTE

The musical text of the 52 sonatas included in this two-volume Dover edition is reprinted, without abridgment or change of sequence, from the three volumes comprising *Serie 14: Klavierwerke*, n.d. [actually 1918; edited by Karl Päsler], of the Breitkopf & Härtel (Leipzig) Haydn complete-works edition inaugurated in 1907 under the general editorship of Eusebius Mandyczewski.[1]

Päsler's edition of the piano sonatas was consistently followed, with regard both to pieces included and to their sequence, by the eminent scholar Anthony van Hoboken in the section ("Gruppe XVI") devoted to the sonatas in his authoritative thematic catalogue of Haydn's works.[2] Thus, the sonata numbers used here are also the "Hoboken numbers" (XVI:1, XVI:2, etc.) of the sonatas, numbers that are more useful for reference than the misleading opus numbers sometimes associated with the pieces. The dates of composition of the sonatas supplied in the present table of contents are those given by Hoboken, not those given by Päsler.

Inasmuch as these two Dover volumes are intended primarily as a convenient and reliable playing edition, certain other types of background information have been intentionally omitted. The (German-language) editorial commentary in the Päsler edition does not appear here, chiefly for reasons of space. No attempt has been made even to summarize the extremely complex publication history of the sonatas, a number of which were in fact originally published in the eighteenth century as the work of other composers and were first attributed to Haydn by Päsler in 1918; the reader interested in these matters should by all means consult Hoboken. For analogous reasons, names of original dedicatees are also omitted here. Moreover, the pieces are uniformly referred to here as sonatas, even though some were originally published with such titles as partita and divertimento.

Nevertheless, despite the intentionally unpedantic approach taken in the present edition, it is only proper to point out that not all 52 sonatas included here are universally accepted as authentic works by Haydn. To take a highly significant instance of dissent, the catalogue of Haydn's works compiled by Georg Feder for the 1980 *New Grove Dictionary of Music and Musicians*[3] considers eleven of the Hoboken/Päsler sonatas as doubtful attributions, and two of them as absolutely spurious; see the Grove article for detailed reasons and suggested reattributions (the dates of composition given in Grove for many of the sonatas also differ from Hoboken's). The 47 sonatas listed in Grove as absolutely authentic include the remaining 39 Hoboken/Päsler sonatas, seven lost works and one fragment included by Hoboken under a different category ("Gruppe XIV," *Divertimenti mit Klavier*).

Following is a three-way concordance of the sonatas making use of the 52 Hoboken "authentic" numbers, the 47 Grove "authentic" numbers and the frequently used 62 WU numbers ("Wiener Urtext," i.e., *J. Haydn: Sämtliche Klaviersonaten*, 3 vols., ed. by C. Landon, Vienna, 1964–66).

---

[1] *Joseph Haydns Werke. Erste kritisch durchgesehene Gesamtausgabe.* In the three-volume *Serie 14*, the first volume contained Sonatas 1–22; the second, 23–38; the third, 39–52.

[2] *Joseph Haydn. Thematisch-bibliographisches Werkverzeichnis zusammengestellt von Anthony van Hoboken*, B. Schott's Söhne, Mainz, 1957.

[3] Edited by Stanley Sadie; Macmillan Publishers Limited, London.

HOBOKEN	GROVE	WU	HOBOKEN	GROVE	WU	HOBOKEN	GROVE	WU	HOBOKEN	GROVE	WU
1	doubtful	10	14	2	16	27	25	42	40	40	54
2	doubtful	11	15	spurious	—	28	26	43	41	41	55
3	3	14	16	doubtful	—	29	27	44	42	42	56
4	4	9	17	spurious	—	30	28	45	43	37	35
5	doubtful	8	18	17	20	31	29	46	44	18	32
6	1	13	19	14	30	32	30	47	45	13	29
7	doubtful	2	20	36	33	33	38	34	46	16	31
8	doubtful	1	21	19	36	34	39	53	47	12	57 (& 19)
9	doubtful	3	22	20	37	35	31	48	48	43	58
10	doubtful	6	23	21	38	36	32	49	49	44	59
11	doubtful	5	24	22	39	37	33	50	50	46	60
12	doubtful	12	25	23	40	38	34	51	51	47	61
13	doubtful	15	26	24	41	39	35	52	52	45	62

GROVE	HOBOKEN	WU	GROVE	HOBOKEN	WU	GROVE	HOBOKEN	WU	GROVE	HOBOKEN	WU
1	6	13	18	44	32	29	31	46	40	40	54
2	14	16	19	21	36	30	32	47	41	41	55
3	3	14	20	22	37	31	35	48	42	42	56
4	4	9	21	23	38	32	36	49	43	48	58
5–11	(lost)	21–27	22	24	39	33	37	50	44	49	59
12	47	57 (& 19)	23	25	40	34	38	51	45	52	62
13	45	29	24	26	41	35	39	52	46	50	60
14	19	30	25	27	42	36	20	33	47	51	61
15	(fragment)	28	26	28	43	37	43	35			
16	46	31	27	29	44	38	33	34			
17	18	20	28	30	45	39	34	53			

WU	HOBOKEN	GROVE	WU	HOBOKEN	GROVE	WU	HOBOKEN	GROVE	WU	HOBOKEN	GROVE
1	8	doubtful	15	13	doubtful	35	43	37	49	36	32
2	7	doubtful	16	14	2	36	21	19	50	37	33
3	9	doubtful	17	—	doubtful	37	22	20	51	38	34
4	doubtful	doubtful	18	—	doubtful	38	23	21	52	39	35
5	11	doubtful	19	—	12(a)	39	24	22	53	34	39
6	10	doubtful	20	18	17	40	25	23	54	40	40
7	—	doubtful	21–27	2 a–h (lost)	5–11	41	26	24	55	41	41
8	5	doubtful	28	(fragment)	15	42	27	25	56	42	42
9	4	4	29	45	13	43	28	26	57	47	12(b)
10	1	doubtful	30	19	14	44	29	27	58	48	43
11	2	doubtful	31	46	16	45	30	28	59	49	44
12	12	doubtful	32	44	18	46	31	29	60	50	46
13	6	1	33	20	36	47	32	30	61	51	47
14	3	3	34	33	38	48	35	31	62	52	45

CONTENTS

The dates are those of composition, as given by Hoboken in his thematic catalogue.

Sonata No. 30 in A Major

Tempo di Menuetto, con Variazioni.

cantabile

Var. I.

Sonata No. 31 in E Major

Sonata No. 32 in B Minor

Tempo di Menuetto.

Menuet.

Men: Da Capo.
(D.C. Maggiore)

Finale.
Presto.

Sonata No. 33 in D Major

Sonata No. 34 in E Minor

Finale.
Molto vivace.

Sonata No. 35 in C Major

Adagio.

Finale.
Allegro.

Sonata No. 36 in C-sharp Minor

Scherzando.
Allegro con brio.

Menuetto da capo.

Sonata No. 37 in D Major

Largo e sostenuto.

Finale.
Presto, ma non troppo.

Innocentemente.

Attacca subito
(il) Finale.

Sonata No. 38 in E-flat Major

Adagio.

attacca subito

Finale.
Allegro.

Da Capo sin al segno

Sonata No. 39 in G Major

Sempre più Largo.

Tempo primo.

Sonata No. 40 in G Major

Presto.

100   Sonata No. 40 in G Major

Sonata No. 41 in B-flat Major

Allegro di molto.

Sonata No. 42 in D Major

Andante con espressione.

Vivace assai.

Sonata No. 43 in A-flat Major

Menuetto I.

Menuetto 2do

Men: I da Capo.

Sonata No. 44 in G Minor

Sonata No. 45 in E-flat Major

Sonata No. 46 in A-flat Major

Finale.
Presto.

Sonata No. 47 in F Major

Larghetto.

(attacca)

Sonata No. 48 in C Major

Andante con espressione.

Sonata No. 49 in E-flat Major

Adagio cantabile.

188   Sonata No. 49 in E-flat Major

Sonata No. 50 in C Major

Adagio.

Allegro molto.

208   Sonata No. 50 in C Major

Sonata No. 51 in D Major

Finale.
Presto.

Sonata No. 52 in E-flat Major